Animal Pranksters

Burrowing Owls

by Julie Murray

2

Dash!
LEVELED READERS
An Imprint of Abdo Zoom • abdobooks.com

Dash! LEVELED READERS 2

Level 1 – Beginning
Short and simple sentences with familiar words or patterns for children who are beginning to understand how letters and sounds go together.

Level 2 – Emerging
Longer words and sentences with more complex language patterns for readers who are practicing common words and letter sounds.

Level 3 – Transitional
More developed language and vocabulary for readers who are becoming more independent.

THIS BOOK CONTAINS RECYCLED MATERIALS

abdobooks.com

Published by Abdo Zoom, a division of ABDO, PO Box 398166, Minneapolis, Minnesota 55439.

Printed in the United States of America, North Mankato, Minnesota.
052022
092022

Photo Credits: Getty Images, Minden Pictures, Shutterstock
Production Contributors: Kenny Abdo, Jennie Forsberg, Grace Hansen, John Hansen
Design Contributors: Candice Keimig, Neil Klinepier

Library of Congress Control Number: 2021950306

Publisher's Cataloging in Publication Data

Names: Murray, Julie, author.
Title: Burrowing owls / by Julie Murray.
Description: Minneapolis, Minnesota : Abdo Zoom, 2023 | Series: Animal pranksters | Includes online resources and index.
Identifiers: ISBN 9781098228330 (lib. bdg.) | ISBN 9781644947609 (pbk.) | ISBN 9781098229177 (ebook) | ISBN 9781098229597 (Read-to-Me ebook)
Subjects: LCSH: Burrowing owl--Juvenile literature. | Owls--Juvenile literature. | Birds--Behavior--Juvenile literature. | Zoology--Juvenile literature.
Classification: DDC 598.9--dc23

Table of Contents

Burrowing Owls

Burrowing owls live in parts of North and South America.

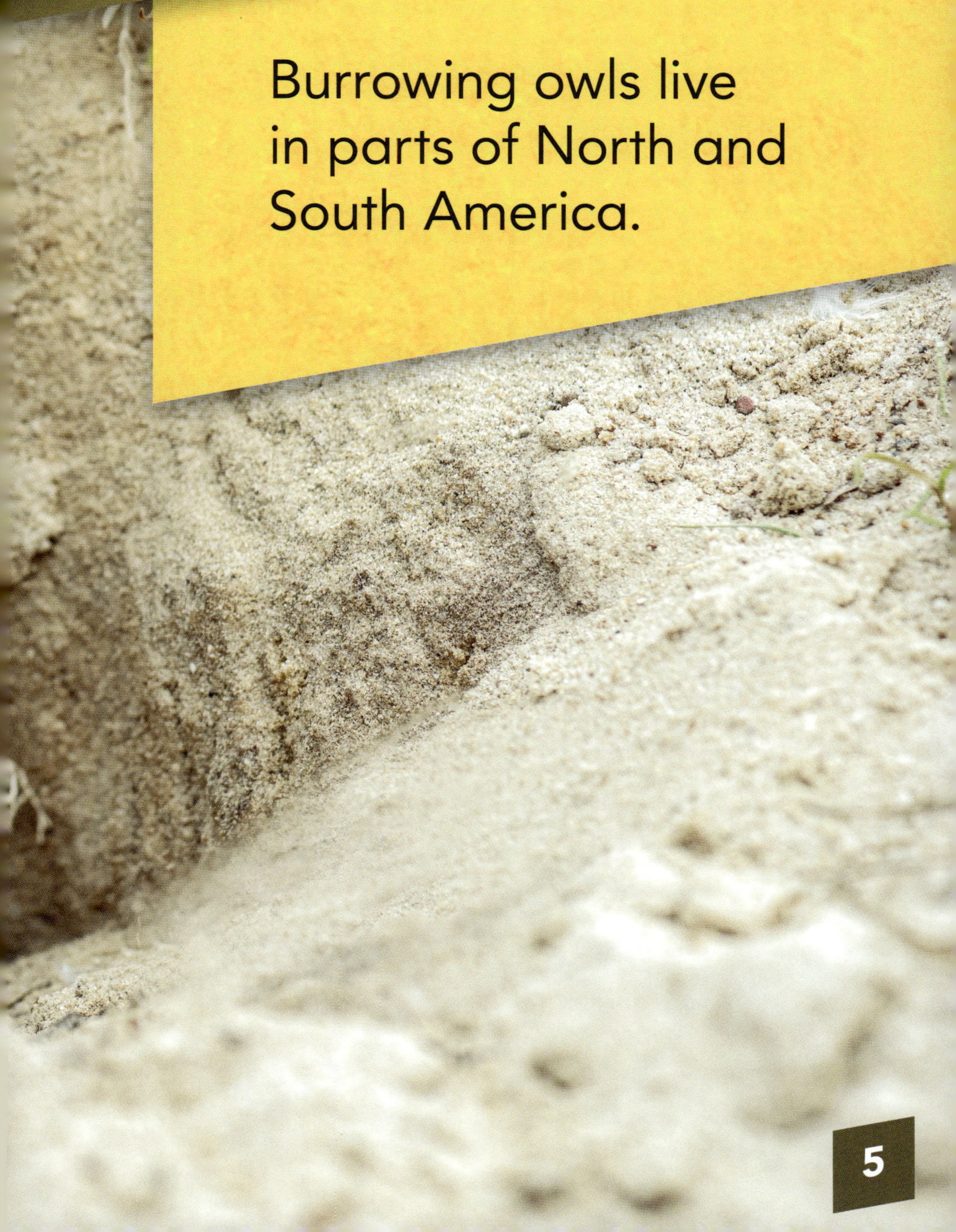

They are found in open areas, like grasslands, prairies, and deserts.

They live in **burrows**. They often use burrows that other animals made and left behind.

They are small owls. They stand 7.5 to 10 inches (19 to 25 cm) tall. They weigh 4.5 to 9 ounces (0.13 to 0.26 kg).

Their feathers are a mix of brown and white. Their eyes and beaks are yellow. Young owls have different coloring.

young burrowing owls

Burrowing owls hunt during the day. They eat small mammals and insects. They also eat frogs and lizards.

Tricking Beetles

Burrowing owls are pranksters! They like to trick **dung beetles**.

They collect animal dung. Then, they lay it around the opening of their **burrow**.

They wait for the beetles to come. Then, they snatch them up for a tasty meal!

More Facts

- Burrowing owls make a rattlesnake sound when they feel threatened. This scares **predators** away.

- Their **burrows** can be ten feet (3.05 m) long. A nesting area is toward the back.

- A female lays 2 to 12 eggs at a time. She sits on the eggs for 30 days until they hatch.

Glossary

burrow – a hole or tunnel dug by certain animals for use as a hiding place or home.

dung beetle – beetles that feed on the droppings of other animals. Dung is the manure of animals.

predator – an animal that hunts other animals for food.

Index

Online Resources

Booklinks
NONFICTION NETWORK
FREE! ONLINE NONFICTION RESOURCES

To learn more about burrowing owls, please visit **abdobooklinks.com** or scan this QR code. These links are routinely monitored and updated to provide the most current information available.